If I had a mas
in Provence . . .

© ÉDITIONS ÉQUINOXE
Domaine de Fontgisclar, Draille de Magne
13570 Barbentane

ISBN 2-84135-231-5
ISSN 1264-4714

Lizzie Napoli

TRANSLATED BY JULIE ROSSINI AND ALISON CROSSLEY

If I had a mas in Provence . . .

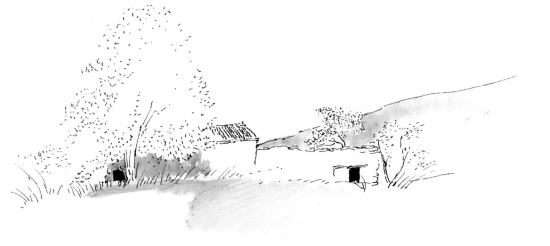

ÉQUIN•XE

If I had a mas
in Provence…

this is a dream shared by many,
especially those who live
in parts of the world where winter
lasts longer than summer.

the following pages describe how "mas"
were built traditionally,
and how to combine old and new
for a harmonious home for today

And, who knows, one day perhaps,
    your dream may come true...

In a landscape
vibrant with sunshine
and pungent with the scent
of lavender and dried herbs

7

_At the end of a path
bordered with Hollyhocks
three cypresses welcome guests ...

9

Dreams are boundless.

A "mas" can also :
— be extended by the addition
of two or three small rooms or sheds,
all built to different heights, as was customary
for the arrival of a child
for a new animal or to house
a new occupation .

_ cling to a rocky outcrop
with buttresses

— or stand on the flat, walls
that are wide at the base and narrower at the top.
a "mas" like this does not need deep foundations.

Nearing the mas

a courtyard,
with a mulberry tree
casting shade
over the stone table
for summer mealtimes

the walls around the courtyard
served as a protection against
mistral winds and brigands

15

Outside floors

Crazy pebble paving
may follow the curve of a wall
or path

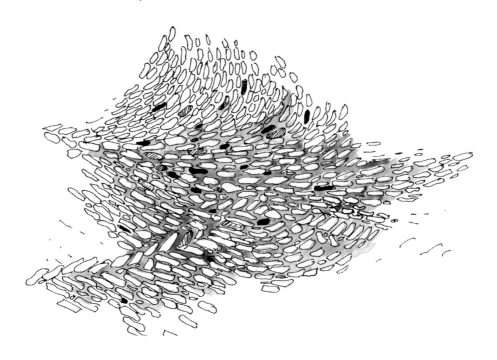

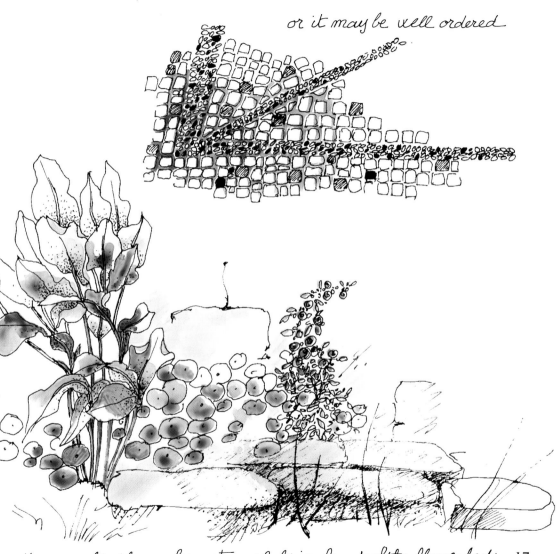

or it may be well ordered

You can also place a few stone slabs in front of the flowerbeds 17

Roofs

When the last tile is in place,
a fossilized sea urchin is thrown on to the roof
to protect the house from lightning.

According to legend, Belshazzar,
one of the three Wise Men,
was journeying through Provence
following the nativity star
when he met a beautiful maiden.
He tarried awhile,
so to remind him of his divine mission,
the star became engraved
on stones all around him
hence the sea urchin ...

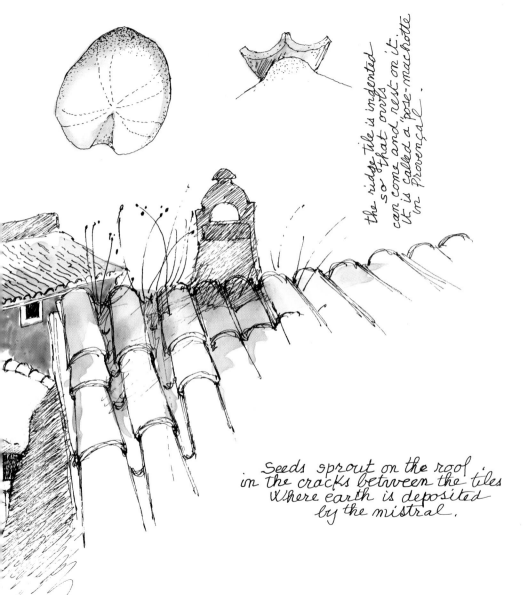

the ridge tile is indented so that owls can come and rest on it. It is called a "pose-machotte" in Provençale.

Seeds sprout on the roof in the cracks between the tiles where earth is deposited by the mistral.

If you want to know how it is done

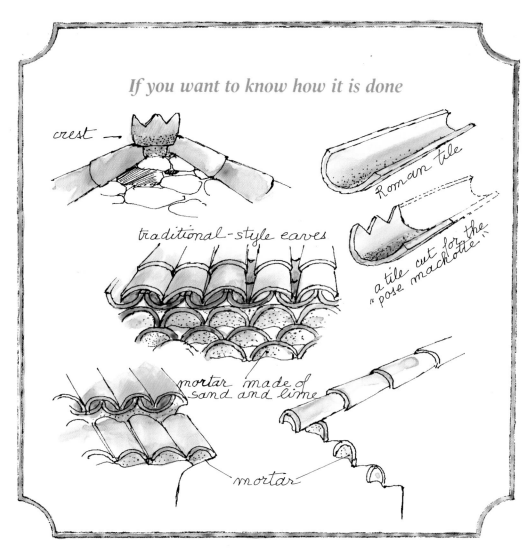

crest

Roman tile

a tile cut for the "pose machotte"

traditional-style eaves

mortar made of sand and lime

mortar

Exterior walls

Exposed stones tended to be used for the outbuildings, barns and sheds, while the buildings were roughcast.

In an exposed stone construction, the stones fit so tightly together that there is practically no need for mortar, like the low drystone walls along country paths.

Whereas when the walls were to be roughcast, the stones were piled up haphazardly with much wider joints as they were never meant to be seen.

exposed stone wall

stones under a roughcast

drystone wall

Ochre

On of the charms of Provence
lies in the warm hues that vary
from village to village.
these range from red ochre
to golden white and saffron yellow,
according to the local terrain.
— In the old days, people would
only use building materials
they could find nearly,
which is why each village still
has its own
distinctive
harmony of
shades.

According to legend,
there was once a
beautiful girl
called Sirmonde
who threw herself from
the high cliffs in
Roussillon
of a broken heart
this is how the land
was stained red
with her blood —

Frontages coating

Façades made of rubble are protected with a coating of sand, water and natural hydrated lime : three coats of this rendering are applied, each thinner than the last, the final coat being "frotassée", that is, lightly grazed with a faggot of rosemary or broom twigs.

— Unlike cement, the lime coating matures with the walls, enabling them to settle and breathe over time — the traditional colour comes from the natural hue of the sand.

80 to 95% of ochrous sand is needed to obtain the remainder in ochre pigments — Extracting the pigment requires loads of ochrous sand, scores of water hoses, channels, successive basins and mixers, hundreds of litres of water, and months of sunshine to dry the ochre that is cut into blocks and piled up to form low walls. It then goes through a maze of mills, crushers, grinders and silk screens so that pure ochre (in its pigment form) can be packed clean and fluid in jar for you to buy to "paint your "mas".

the sand reddens when heated to between 400 and 700°C.

23

Conservatory of ochre and applied pigments

Ochre from local cliffs was extracted for about 200 years until chemical pigments were invented. The Mathieu factory founded at the beginning of the century and almost fully restored today is a testimony of our heritage. Although it no longer produces ochre commercially, it still operates from February to November for the benefit of visitors. It is also a place where artisans and professionals can meet and share their skills with the public. The Mathieu ochre factory also offers workshops on other natural dyes sold in their shop.

madder
heather
indigo
campeachy wo
curcuma
pastel
aloe
ultramarin
sienna
umber
benzoin
spermaceti:
judea bitume
etc...

Not so long ago, people would distemper
their façades for Easter.

Distemper =
whitewash
i.e.
water + lime
paste
pigment.

In France
paste is made from
dairy product, whereas
in the East, they use rice
and in Scandinavia,
wheat.

Sundials

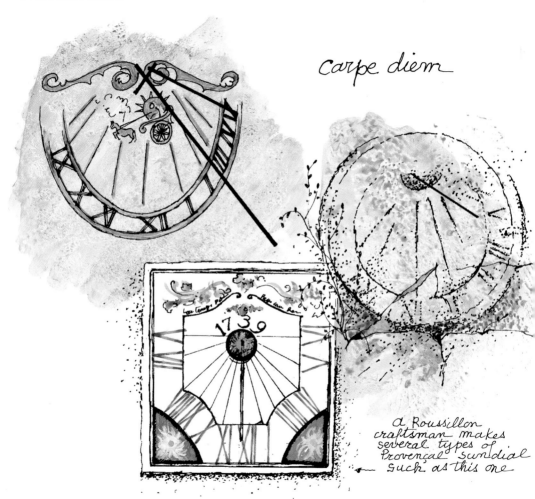

carpe diem

a Roussillon craftsman makes several types of Provençal sundial such as this one

the sun gives us its joy, beauty
and warmth.
— It may also show us the time
In Provence there is always a
south - facing wall, where the face
of a sundial can be painted.
Graduating the hours
is not easy, though...
— the shadow of the iron pin or "style",
shows the time if it is set in the right
place and properly inclined —

— And even with a handbook for
setting sundials, it is hard not to
get lost between the latitudes
meridians, zenithal heights etc...

While awaiting successful
completion, you'll have plenty of time
to think up a motto for your sundial.

Here is mine → (BE LIKE ME
ONLY MARK
THE HOURS OF THE SUN)

27

28

Woodwork colours

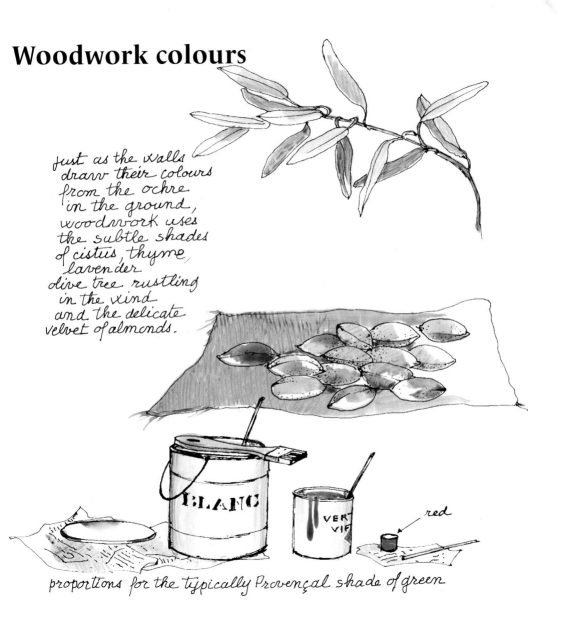

Just as the walls draw their colours from the ochre in the ground, woodwork uses the subtle shades of cistus, thyme, lavender dive tree rustling in the wind and the delicate velvet of almonds.

BLANC

VERT VIF

red

proportions for the typically Provençal shade of green

Small openings

there is often a small window
at the top of the "mas",
      like an eye
         for viewing
   the surrounding landscape
      and small
   to let light into the loft,
   while protecting a harvest
      from sun and wind.

or provide shelter
for a stray bird.

31

The door

Often framed by a vine or a "wisteria", almost always made of solid wood, but typical of Provence with its four panes of glass to let the sunlight stream in.

Sometimes there is also an outer, hinged mosquito screen

Or even a bead
curtain that jingles
whenever someone
comes or goes,
creating musical
memories
for wintertime.

The entrance

Inside the door,
the traditional Provençal
three-seater welcomes you.

In many "mas", the door still
opens onto a small,
square entrance hall.

A door on the left leads
to where the sheep lived
another on the right
to the labourers' room
and a large kitchen
and opposite,
a staircase
led up
to the bedrooms.

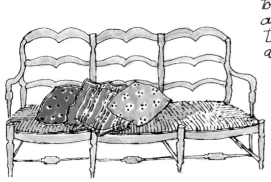

Nowadays, sadly, there are far less sheep,
and they are usually kept apart from the
house, in separate sheds.

And the stairs have often been moved
to make a more spacious entrance hall...

Other fortunate "mas" owners have an old, outdoor, stone staircase leading up to a loft where hay, grapes and beans could be kept to dry.

35

Space

Domesticated down the centuries
shaped by everyday life,
the volumes have finally
reached a state of harmony.

Whereas modifying the façade
is an awkward business,
it is possible to open up vistas
from one room to another.
Even if the opening is small it will
create an illusion of new perspectives.

A space should be beautiful
on its own. It cannot be improved
by the addition of objects.

You must always be able to imagine
that there is still something else
to discover behind the door
on the other side of the wall,
beyond the terrace,
over the hill,
at the end of one's life...

so the dream never ends...

How to put in openings

_ First, draw the outline on the wall
you want to open to better visualise it.
If it is only a small opening star carefully
with a hammer and chisel (the stones are
precious, and they are often softer than mortar).

If you are planning a larger opening,
call in a professional (it will be
much less tiring...), who can tell you
if you need to reinforce the opening,
and if so, whether it would be better
to use a stone lintel or a beam.

_ If it is a partition wall, it will not be thicker
than 8 cm, and it will be made of plaster
You can use a handsaw (that will be
ruined in the process), to cut it out
yourself, as plaster is not heavy and does
not leave rubble.
_ You can then smooth edges
with fresh plaster (see p 44)

Inside floors

"Mas" are generally paved with clay
tiles or bricks fired reddish-brown
in very hot kilns.

When "mas" were built
near quarries, stone slabs were used. 39

Ceilings

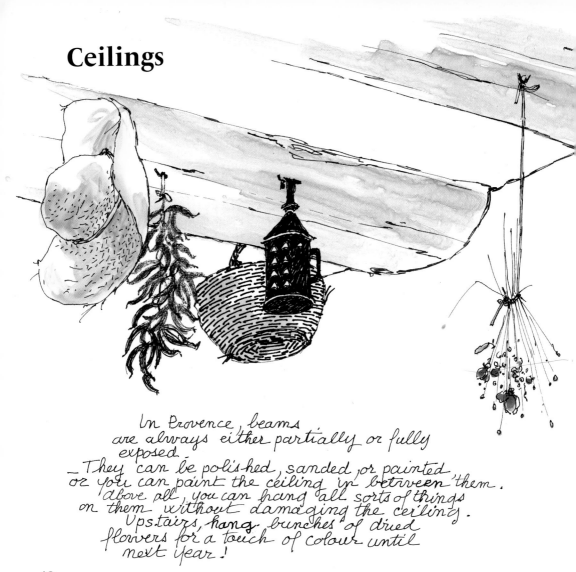

In Provence, beams
are always either partially or fully
exposed.
_They can be polished, sanded or painted
or you can paint the ceiling in between them.
Above all, you can hang all sorts of things
on them without damaging the ceiling.
Upstairs, hang bunches of dried
flowers for a touch of colour until
next year!

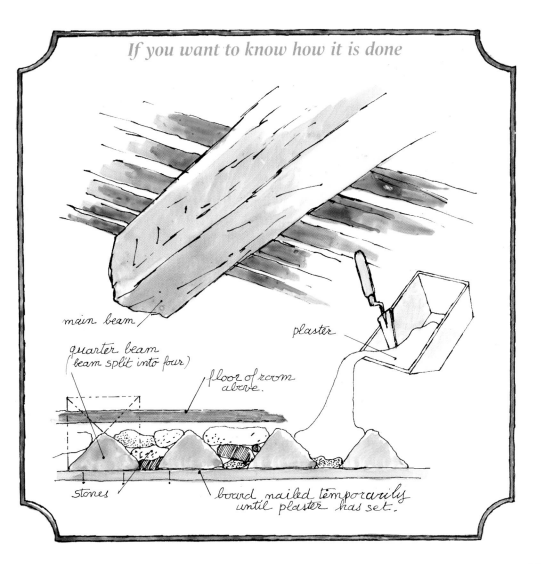

main beam

quarter beam
(beam split into four)

floor of room
above.

plaster

stones

board nailed temporarily
until plaster has set.

A step

not necessarily for going up or down,
it can be used to display things,
as a seat, or, if it is wide enough
as a spare bed for an unexpected
friend.

— If you are optimistic or valiant enough
to plan on doing some studious work
in Provence you can spread out your
files here that, if left piled up on a
desk or a table, might not get
opened — except maybe the top one — and
would certainly look untidy if left
on the floor!...

It might be your only chance to find a use
for the cup your grandfather won and you
do not want to throw away. It will hold
your papers in place when the mistral
comes whistling through the open door.

Or maybe this flat iron a friend
spent weeks polishing, in the days
when you had no electricity!...

URGENT

42

How to build a step

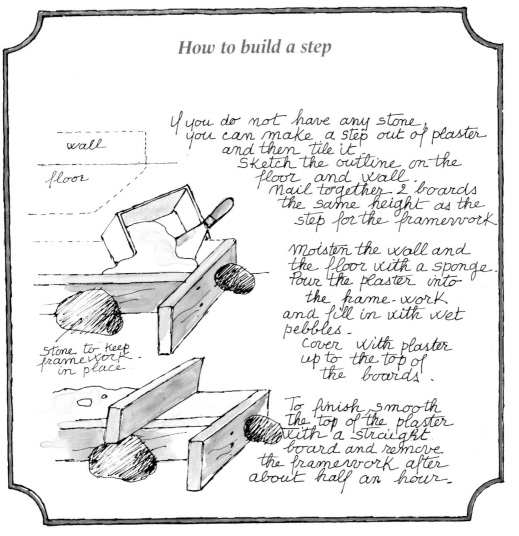

wall

floor

If you do not have any stone, you can make a step out of plaster and then tile it.
Sketch the outline on the floor and wall.
Nail together 2 boards the same height as the step for the framework.

Moisten the wall and the floor with a sponge.
Pour the plaster into the frame-work and fill in with wet pebbles.
Cover with plaster up to the top of the boards.

To finish, smooth the top of the plaster with a straight board and remove the framework after about half an hour.

stone to keep framework in place.

How to make plaster

Plaster is the material that best suits our white walls in Provence.

— You can create curves or angles using just this white powder and a little water for a very modest sum.

It's white, it's neat,
it's easy to keep clean.
You can display things on it.
It stays warm for several hours:
it's as if it were alive.
And if you make e mistake, you can break it up and start again!

It's magic!

for small DIY projects buy small 2 oz 5¼ buy bag of plaster in hardware or DIY stores.

Also buy two 6 cm. knives (like the palette.

(like these).

< 6 cm >

protect your clothes

lay newspapers (without reading them!)

always moisten the area where you are going to apply plaster

Sprinkle the same quantity of plaster and water in a plastic basin. — Stir once then wait for the plaster to set for 10 minutes. It is now ready to use.

Put some plaster on a palette knife, and smooth it from one knife to the other to keep it soft and moist.

Is the cake baked yet?

If you want to undertake a major project and you are no Hercules, invite a brawny neighbour, friend or soulmate for tea. While the cake is baking or too hot to eat take him to the local supplier of building materials and buy 40 kg bags of plaster of Paris. It's much cheaper than the plaster used for repair works.

Fireplaces

A log fire brings a bit of sunshine to a rainy day (it does sometimes rain here!) Since man discovered fire, he has always gathered round it for protection for warmth, and for holding profound conversations...

All you need to know to really take advantage of a fireplace

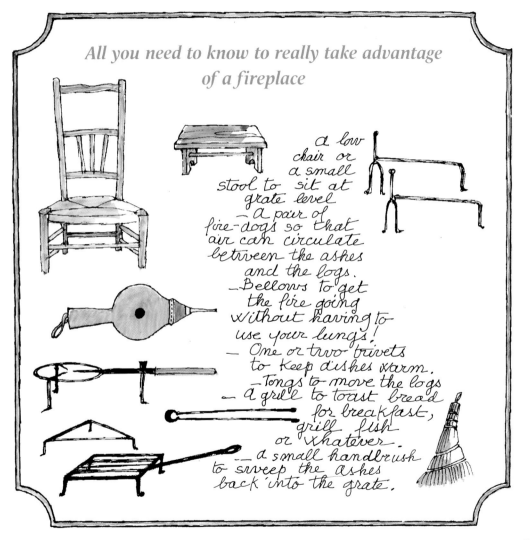

a low chair or a small stool to sit at grate level
— A pair of fire-dogs so that air can circulate between the ashes and the logs.
— Bellows to get the fire going without having to use your lungs!
— One or two trivets to keep dishes warm.
— Tongs to move the logs
— a grill to toast bread for breakfast, grill fish or whatever.
— a small handbrush to sweep the ashes back into the grate.

It is also near the fireplace that santons are displayed.
— On Sainte Barbe's day, on 4th December, wheat, barley and corn seeds as well as chickpeas and lentils are placed to sprout in a dish.
On Christmas Day, the sprouts are tall and green, ready to decorate the crib.

48

In the crib, you need first of all
   Baby Jesus
  the Virgin Mary and Joseph
  the donkey and the ox
         then the shepherd and his sheep
         the three Wise Men
         the simpleton
         the country policeman
         Law
         Old Age
         innocence
And every year, you can add one or two more
typical Provençal characters. It is all part
of the fun of Christmas shopping.

Hoods

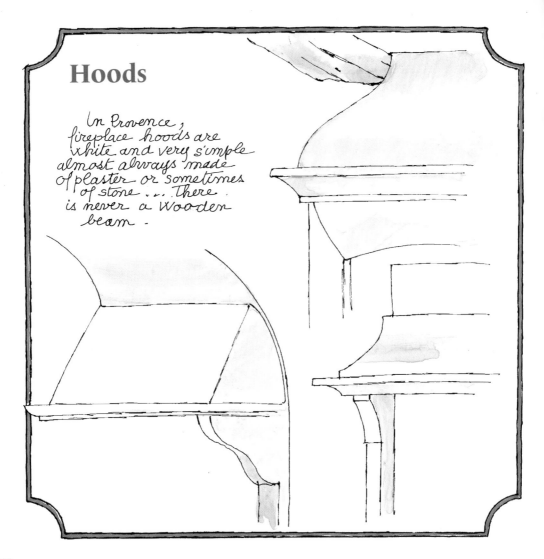

In Provence,
fireplace hoods are
white and very simple
almost always made
of plaster or sometimes
of stone ... There
is never a wooden
beam.

The "potager"

Usually very close to the fireplace, and sometimes even inside it. When the fireplace is large. In any case it is always in the same room. Everywhere else in France, the word "potager" means vegetable garden., but in Provence, it is a place to put hot embers to keep a dish warm.

Details of a "potager"

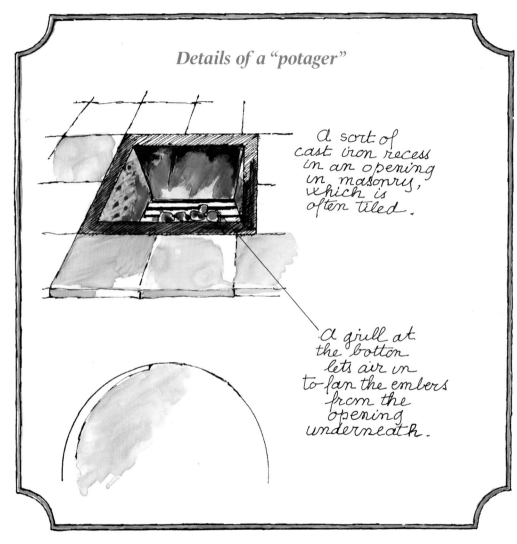

A sort of cast iron recess in an opening in masonry, which is often tiled.

A grill at the bottom lets air in to fan the embers from the opening underneath.

Niches

The vinegar cruet niche

the thick Provençal
walls mean
all sorts of niches that
can be hollowed out
to safely display
and protect
your vinegar cruet...

a vinegar cruet
should not be placed
in a draught, and it doesn't like
being moved around.
— Calculate the right height
for your niche so that there is
no need for you to move the cruet
when you add wine or to draw out vinegar.
— the tap should protrude from
the niche so that vinegar can drip
into a bowl placed underneath.

53

The draining niche

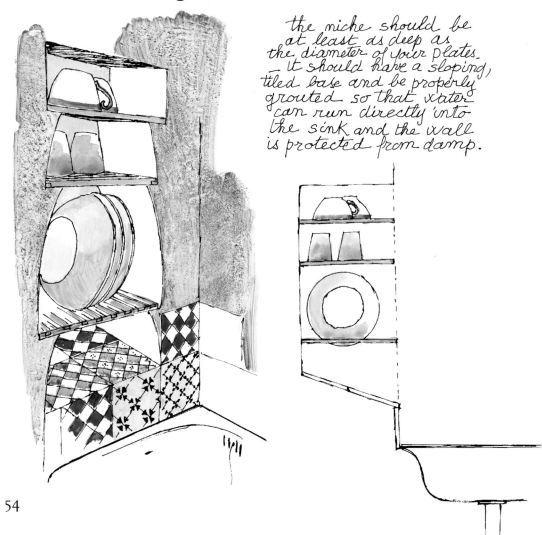

the niche should be
at least as deep as
the diameter of your plates.
It should have a sloping,
tiled base and be properly
grouted so that water
can run directly into
the sink and the wall
is protected from damp.

How to make the wickers for this niche

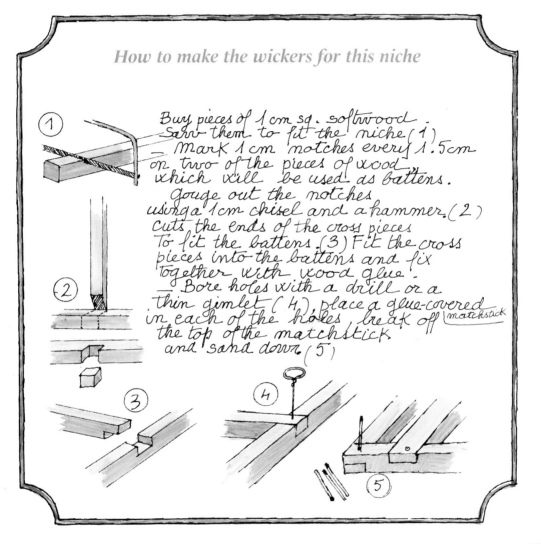

Buy pieces of 1 cm sq. softwood. Saw them to fit the niche (1)
- Mark 1 cm notches every 1.5cm on two of the pieces of wood which will be used as battens.
Gouge out the notches using a 1cm chisel and a hammer. (2)
Cuts the ends of the cross pieces To fit the battens. (3) Fit the cross pieces into the battens and fix Together with wood glue.
- Bore holes with a drill or a thin gimlet (4) place a glue-covered matchstick in each of the holes, break off the top of the matchstick and sand down. (5)

matchstick

The shelf niche

Have fun choosing arranging and displaying your favourite objects.

How to hide brackets

To put up shelves in a niche or a blocked-up doorway, all you need to do is nail battens at the same height on either side and put the shelves in place. The shelves will look part of the wall if you cover the battens with plaster.

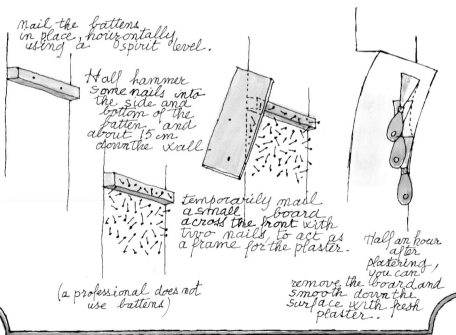

nail the battens in place, horizontally using a spirit level.

Half hammer some nails into the side and bottom of the batten, and about 15 cm down the wall.

temporarily nail a small board across the front with two nails, to act as a frame for the plaster.

(a professional does not use battens)

Half an hour after plastering, you can remove the board and smooth down the surface with fresh plaster.

57

you can build shelves in the middle of a room or along a wall, using plaster slabs sawn to the right size, and assembled. the size of the shelves will vary according to wat you want to display books, a television set, a dolls' house, a fish bowl, a serving basket, a lamp etc.

if you want to make shelves longer than the plaster slabs thick dark wood, looks good. with white plaster.

58

small, ready-made
shelves and cupboards
may not be antique,
but still look
charming against
a white wall.

"Panetières"

(the piece of furniture where bread used to be kept)

Classic "panetière" can be found at antique dealers'.

Catholic "panetière"

protestant "panetière"

Place settings holders and glass holders

these ones
made of
earthenware
can be seen
at the museon
Arlaten, founded
in 1896 by
Frédéric Mistral
in Arles.
they could
inspire today's
potters.

The radassière

From "radasso" in Provençal:
to idle or lounge about.

Originally, it came from Turkey and meant
the Turkish divan in
the ceremonial chamber.

the privileged few would recline on piles
of cushions at the back of an alcove occupying
the full width of the room watching
dancers... In Provence, it is more a place
to relax, to gossip or to doze during
the hottest hours of the day.

the "radassière" is a wooden frame
running right along the length of one wall.
it is covered with a mattress of the
same size and lots of cushions!

In the middle of the wall, a window
lets sunlight filter in through the shutters
followed by lengthening shadows
and dusk...

Television sets have perhaps
replaced the dancers...?

the "radassière" is mostly covered
in Provençal fabrics.

Provençal fabrics

Up to the 17th century, cotton fabrics were decorated using woodcuts and natural dyes, like the indispensable madder. The small dye-mills have gone, replaced by industrial printing works, but they still use the old woodcut motifs.

woodcut

65

A few pieces of furniture from Provence

Provençal furniture
is often painted
in nature's
cheerful colours.

In the bookcase
the books are
protected from
dust by
a screen of
wire netting
— the wire netting
is made of brass wire
drawn through a
draw-plate.

Wardrobes are
wonderful things.
you can open and
close the doors,
have fun with
the drawers,
put things away,
pile up freshly
folded linen,
hide away
precious souvenirs.

Your need a very spacious
room to accommodate a
wardrobe, even if it is
pleasing seen from
all sides!

If you do not
have enough room,
you could use
fine doors on
a fitted cupboard.
They will give
just as much
pleasure, and
take up less space.

It is important
that the inside
be as precious
as the lining
of an Oriental chest.

How to line an armoire

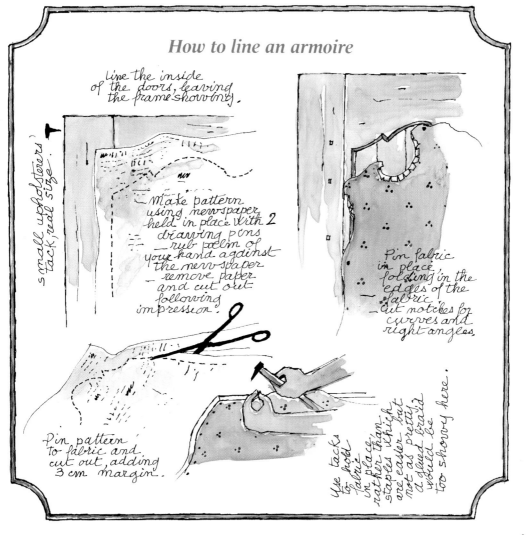

Line the inside of the doors, leaving the frame showing.

small upholsterers' tack, real size.

Make pattern using newspaper held in place with 2 drawing pins — rub palm of your hand against the newspaper — remove paper and cut out following impression.

Pin fabric in place folding in the edges of the fabric — cut notches for curves and right angles.

Pin pattern to fabric and cut out, adding 3 cm margin.

Use tacks to hold fabric in place rather than staples which are easier but not as pretty. A glued braid would be too showy here.

Place
lavender bobbins
on a pile of linen
in the wardrobe.

70

How to tie a lavender bobbin

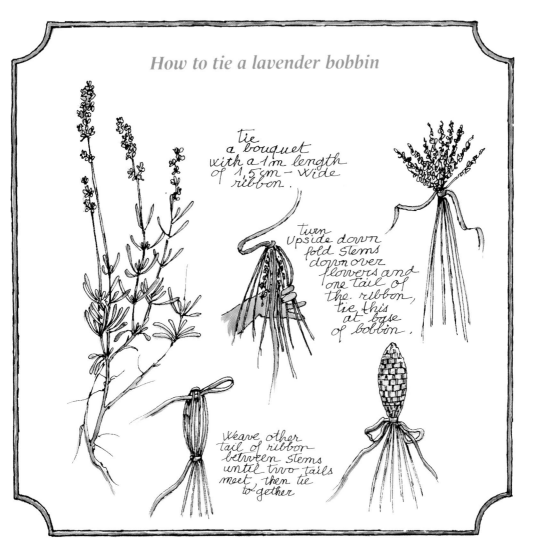

tie a bouquet with a 1m length of 1,5cm-wide ribbon.

turn upside down fold stems down over flowers and one tail of the ribbon, tie this at base of bobbin.

Weave other tail of ribbon between stems until two tails meet, then tie together

Bedrooms

Put your bed in the most secluded
and uppermost room in the "mas"
leave the bustle downstairs
to steal some time for yourself
and enjoy your haven of
peace and quiet,
dreams or passion.

Knowing the room
around you is so beautiful
makes every awakening
a delight.

a bed should be
attractive and
beckon to be unmade...

73

Quilts and "boutis"

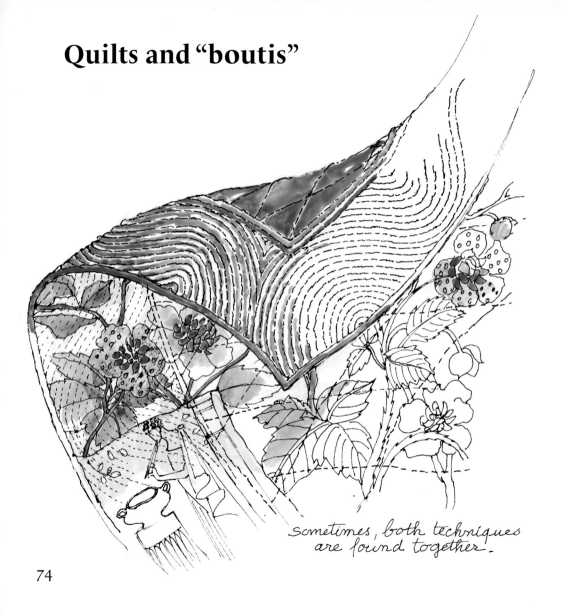

sometimes, both techniques
are found together.

How to know the difference

Quilting and boutis both appeared in the 17th century in Provence but they are two totally different techniques:

— quilting comprises three layers of fabric, one for the lining, one for the padding, and a beautiful printed calico on top. the three layers are sewn together with a tiny running stitch following a broad pattern, as the calico already has a motif.

— boutis (almost always white) is made of two layers only and it is stitching that defines the pattern.
the background, made of closely stitched parallel lines, is highlighted with a twist of cotton inserted with a needle between each row of running stitch. For the motifs — flowers, grapes, and so on —
— the padding is introduced by drawing aside the threads on the wrong side of the fabric using little wooden pegs called "boutis".

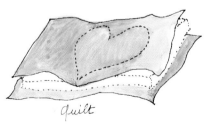

quilt

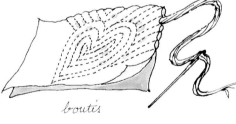

boutis

the printed calicoes, also originally printed using woodcuts, were brought by boat from India and China to Marseilles by the Compagnie des Indes, which had been created by Colbert. For two centuries, the Provençal craftsmen made and exported their quilted bedspreads throughout Europe. Later on, the Provençal people created their own patterns.

Children corner

Prayer for a Provençal newborn:

- May you be as full as an egg,
  as full as an egg,
  May you always have excellent health ...

- May you be as good as bread,
  as good as bread,
  May you always do good.

- May you be as pure as salt,
  as pure as salt,
  May you always be fair.

- May you be as straight as a match,
  as straight as a match,
  May you always be honest.

Bathroom

While you are waiting
for your luxury bath tub,
think of Madame Bonnard,
posing all day long
one foot or shoulder in
a washbowl while
Bonnard painted his
masterpieces.

a bathroom can also be
a living room.

the "soleillant"
is a small room
at the top of the "mas",
protected from the wind,
but open to the elements.
You can sunbathe
peacefully there,
with only the birds and angels
to watch over you.
You can also hang
the washing up there to dry
on rainy days.

The "soleillants"

or you can
gaze at the stars,
if you cannot see the
white horseman riding
over the hill.

Terraces

the word itself can start
      you daydreaming ...
Every time of the day has its own
      special charm:
          — breakfast in the morning
          — making a tart for dessert
          — tea-time
          — needlework in the cool of the evening
          — gazing at the full moon —

A south-facing terrace is shaded by vine arbours.

83

Climbing plants
for the vine arbour

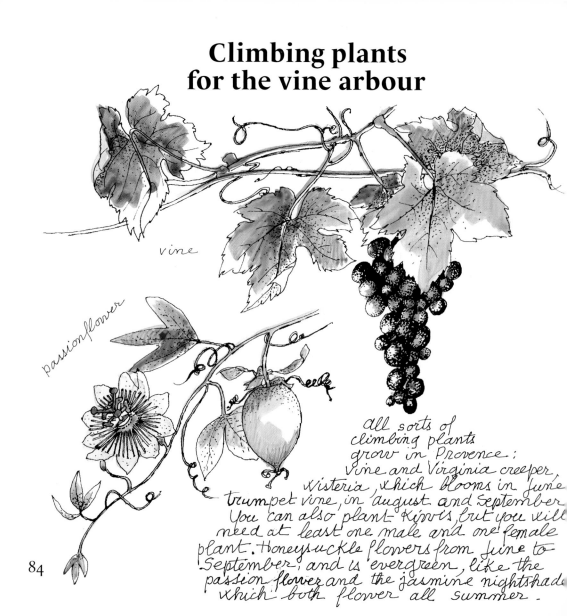

vine

passionflower

All sorts of
climbing plants
grow in Provence:
Vine and Virginia creeper,
Wisteria, which blooms in June,
trumpet vine, in August and September.
You can also plant kiwis, but you will
need at least one male and one female
plant. Honeysuckle flowers from June to
September, and is evergreen, like the
passion flower and the jasmine nightshade
which both flower all summer.

Wisteria

Honeysuckle

85

The nymphée

Why not build a rock grotto
with an outdoor shower
for hot summer days?

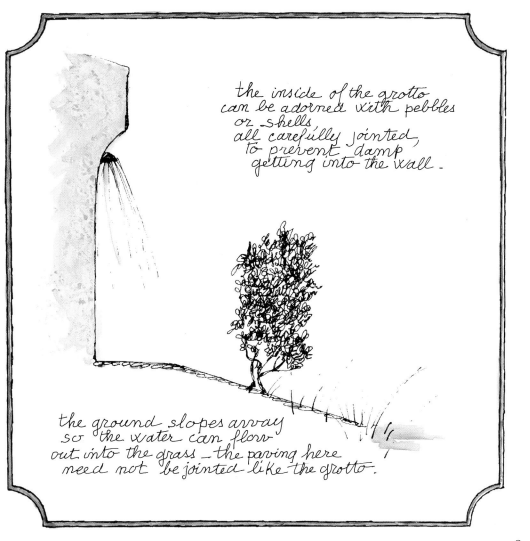

the inside of the grotto
can be adorned with pebbles
or shells
all carefully jointed,
to prevent damp
getting into the wall.

the ground slopes away
so the water can flow
out into the grass — the paving here
need not be jointed like the grotto.

In the garden

Run and pick some herbs to flavour a dish
from your herb garden right by the terrasse.
— It can be planted like a patchwork quilt,
with different herbs in each square. The squares
can be edged with box or with something
more rustic. You can also make paths out of
bricks or pebbles, so as not to get your feet wet
in winter.
— You can replace the squares by triangles,
or any other fancy design...

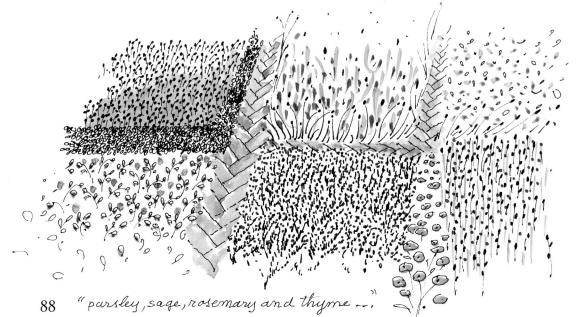

88   " parsley, sage, rosemary and thyme ..."

Rosemary

thyme

Dill

Basil

Sage

garlic

89

Kitchen garden

French beans

courgettes

melon

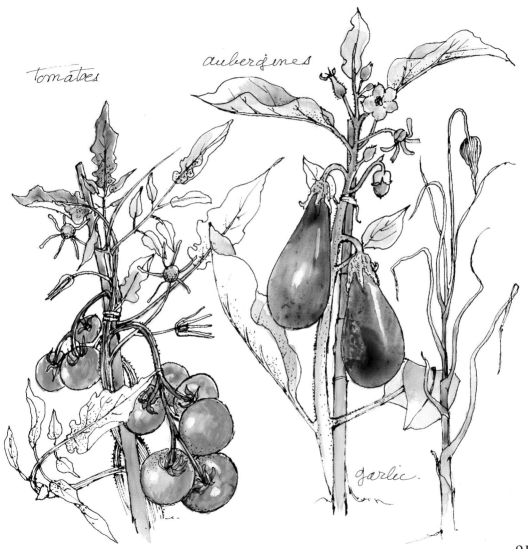

tomatoes

aubergines

garlic.

91

And so the days pass by in the south . . .

Table of contents

Achevé d'imprimer l'été de l'an 2000,
sur les presses de l'imprimerie Grafiche Zanini,
Bologna, Italia.